Alexander Graham Bell
An Inventive Life

written by Elizabeth MacLeod

Kids Can Press

For Yuri, as curious, creative and generous
as Alexander Graham Bell and so deeply missed.

Acknowledgments

Many thanks to the following people who reviewed the book and made such helpful suggestions. At the Alexander Graham Bell National Historic Site: Aynsley MacFarlane, Manager; Anne MacRae, Supervisor of Guide Services; Sharon Morrow, Public Relations; Linda Watson, Heritage Presentation. At the Bell Homestead National Historic Site: Brian Wood, Curator. At Parks Canada, Halifax, Nova Scotia: Denise Hansen, Interpretive Assistant; Terry Shaw, Interpretation Specialist; Judith Tulloch, Historian. I really appreciate the time you took to comment so carefully and thoughtfully.

Thanks to the entire Kids Can Press team, especially Ricky and Valerie. Special thanks to editor Val Wyatt for shaping the book so wonderfully and taking care of the many details with good humor always; designer Karen Powers for the terrific and imaginative look she has given the book; photo researcher Patricia Buckley for her tenacity, dedication and organization and illustrator Barbara Spurll for bringing AGB to life. And always much love and thanks to Paul.

Kids Can Press acknowledges the financial support of the Ontario Arts Council, the Canada Council for the Arts and the Government of Canada, through the BPIDP, for our publishing activity.

Published in Canada by
Kids Can Press Ltd.
29 Birch Avenue
Toronto, ON M4V 1E2

Published in the U.S. by
Kids Can Press Ltd.
2250 Military Road
Tonawanda, NY 14150

www.kidscanpress.com

Edited by Valerie Wyatt
Designed by Karen Powers
Printed and bound in China

The hardcover edition of this book is smyth sewn casebound.
The paperback edition of this book is limp sewn with a drawn-on cover.

CM   99 0 9 8 7 6 5 4 3
CM PA 99 0 9 8 7 6

Canadian Cataloguing in Publication Data

MacLeod, Elizabeth
    Alexander Graham Bell : an inventive life

Includes index.

ISBN-13: 978-1-55074-456-9 (bound)   ISBN-10: 1-55074-456-9 (bound)
ISBN-13: 978-1-55074-458-3 (pbk.)   ISBN-10: 1-55074-458-5 (pbk.)

1. Bell, Alexander Graham, 1847-1922 – Juvenile literature.
2. Inventors – United States – Biography – Juvenile literature.
3. Inventors – Canada – Biography – Juvenile literature.
I. Title.

TK6143.B4M32 1999   j621.38'5092   C98-931616-5

Kids Can Press is a *l'orus*™ Entertainment company

Contents

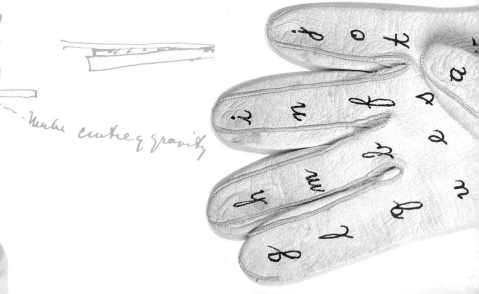

Meet Alexander Graham Bell

Next time you pick up the phone to call a friend or order a pizza, say thanks to Alexander Graham Bell. More than a hundred and twenty-five years ago, he invented the telephone, and his invention changed the world. But the telephone was just one of many accomplishments in his long and inventive life. Alexander Graham Bell, or AGB for short, set records for flight and water speed, helped make *National Geographic* one of the most popular magazines in the world, improved the phonograph (record player), and invented everything from metal probes and air conditioners to water purifiers and iceberg detectors.

An inventor, said AGB, "can no more help inventing than he can help thinking or breathing." For AGB inventing was a way to help people live more safely and comfortably. But where did he get his ideas? And what was he really like?

Over the years phones have gone from big and cumbersome to light and portable. AGB would have been amazed by this cordless cell phone.

AGB knew that tetrahedrons (pyramid shapes) are stable and strong. He used them to make towers and kites and even designed a chair based on them.

Many of AGB's inventions, such as this kite, began with very simple ideas.

One of my rules of inventing is listen to children. They might have ideas we've never thought of.

Once when AGB visited a school, some of the younger kids thought he was Santa Claus. "The children were much puzzled to know how so big a body could come down so small a chimney," AGB wrote to his wife. "I taught them the word 'squeeze' so that they will never forget it!!!"

First Experiments

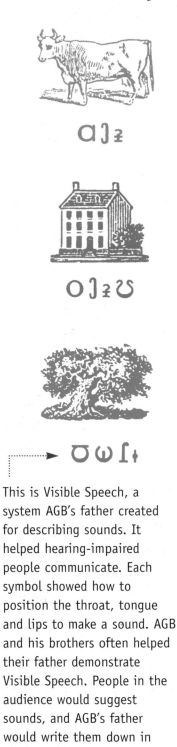

This is Visible Speech, a system AGB's father created for describing sounds. It helped hearing-impaired people communicate. Each symbol showed how to position the throat, tongue and lips to make a sound. AGB and his brothers often helped their father demonstrate Visible Speech. People in the audience would suggest sounds, and AGB's father would write them down in Visible Speech. Then the boys would be called in and asked to read the Visible Speech symbol and make the sound. It could be a word, a bird call or a sound they'd never heard — and they were rarely wrong!

There was that baby crying again! The wailing seemed to come from the Bells' apartment, but the neighbors knew the Bells had no baby. The source of the sound was a machine that young AGB and his brothers had invented. It made such a realistic crying sound that it fooled the neighbors. Even as a child AGB was fascinated by sounds and inventing.

AGB was born in Edinburgh, Scotland, on March 3, 1847. He was the middle boy in a family of three. Early on, he and his brothers, Melville and Edward, began experimenting with sound. In their teens, the boys helped their father demonstrate a system of making sounds based on visual symbols.

When he was 15, AGB's parents sent him to London to study with his grandfather. He learned a lot and discussed sound and electricity with the famous scientists he met there. AGB even learned to massage his dog's vocal cords so that it seemed to say, "How are you, Grandmama?" Later, he taught at a school for hearing-impaired children and studied at the University of London.

By the time AGB was 23, tragedy had struck his family: both his brothers were dead from tuberculosis, a lung disease. Then AGB became sick. His father had spent time in Canada and remembered how clean the air was there. To save AGB's life, the Bells left for Canada on July 21, 1870.

AGB's mother was hearing impaired and sometimes used an ear tube to amplify sound — you can see it in her lap.

That's me at 11. I wasn't a particularly good student. Surprised?

In 1858 AGB posed with his class at Edinburgh Royal High School.

AGB's parents met when his mother painted a picture of his father. His mother also painted this picture of AGB (right) and his brothers Melly (left) and Ted (middle) in 1850, when AGB was three.

The thunder roared,
The rain it poured,
My cottage stood quite strong.
The wind it blew,
Right through and through
Then stopped short —
like this song.

— AGB, age 11

Here is AGB (left) with his father, Alexander Melville Bell (middle), and grandfather, Alexander Bell (right). His father and grandfather both taught people how to speak properly. AGB was originally named Alexander Bell, but when he was 11, a Canadian friend of his parents named Alexander Graham visited. Aleck, as AGB's family called him, decided to add Graham to his name.

Hello, Canada!

The Bells arrived in Canada on August 1, 1870, and soon were settled at a farm on the outskirts of Brantford in southwestern Ontario. Because they had no farming experience, they often turned to their neighbors for help and advice.

The Bells' neighbors thought AGB was a handsome young man but felt sorry for him. They noticed that he spent hours singing into the piano and listening to the vibrations, and they wondered if he was a bit slow. In fact, AGB was experimenting with how sounds travel. He also experimented with a system to collect rainwater and pipe it to the bathroom, and the Bells had the first shower in the area!

AGB's father earned money lecturing about his system of Visible Speech and giving recitals. AGB probably performed, too. When he wasn't helping his father, he visited friends. He didn't have a proper evening suit, but his best friend did. So they shared it — each took a turn staying home while the other wore the suit to neighbors' parties.

The Bell home was on the banks of the Grand River. AGB found a hollow in the riverbank and lined it with blankets and pillows. He spent hours there resting and thinking, mostly about sound and electricity. Gradually his health improved.

Interest in Visible Speech picked up, and soon AGB's father was traveling around North America demonstrating how it worked. When he was asked to teach hearing-impaired children in Boston, he was too busy to take the job and suggested that AGB go instead. AGB left for Boston in March 1871.

AGB became interested in the Mohawk people living near Brantford. He learned to speak their language and recorded it in his father's Visible Speech symbols. In return the Mohawks made AGB an honorary member of their tribal group. He was allowed to wear Mohawk clothing and was taught the Mohawk war dance.

This is the master parlor in the Bells' home in Brantford. AGB once held a test of the telephone here.

If my friends in Scotland could see me now!

AGB loved to play chess. When he and his family went into Brantford, he would play chess with a friend who lived there while his family went off visiting. To save time, he hooked up a buzzer system so that his family could signal when they were ready to head home.

Aleck Bell, Teacher

Georgie Sanders was born hearing impaired and began lessons with AGB in 1872, at age five. AGB wrote books for Georgie to teach him to read and spelled out the alphabet on a glove so Georgie could point to letters and "talk" with people.

AGB was a great success at the Boston School for Deaf Mutes, thanks to his father's Visible Speech and his own teaching methods. He also taught private students and other teachers and gave many lectures on speech.

In October 1873 AGB began teaching at Boston University as professor of Vocal Physiology and Elocution (physiology is the study of how living things function, and elocution is the art of speaking clearly and with expression). To help his students, he used a device called a phonautograph. When a student spoke into the phonautograph, the sound vibrated a thin skin at the other end. The vibrating skin moved a thin rod, which traced a pattern on a piece of smoked glass. Because students could "see" their speech, AGB hoped they could also learn to improve it.

AGB was always trying to find new ways to help his students communicate. But he never missed a chance to talk about sound and electricity with the many scientists who lived in Boston. And he often stayed up well past midnight experimenting with sound.

In-genius invention, if I do say so myself!

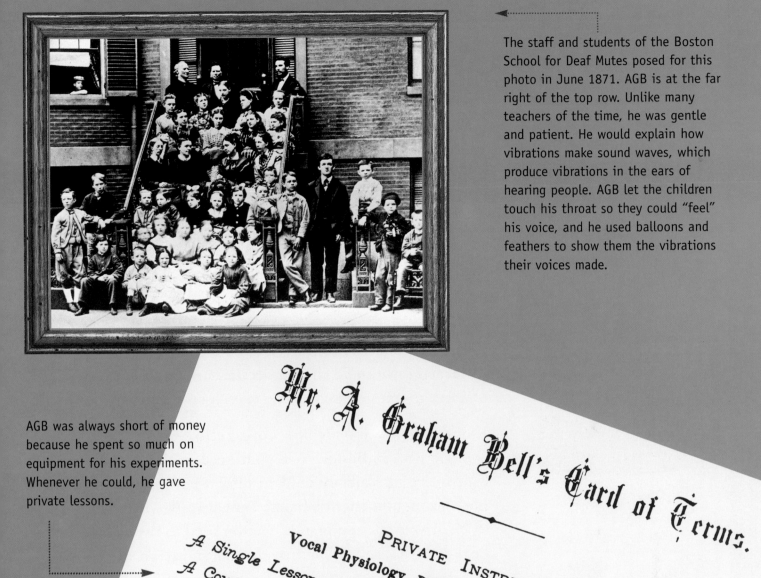

The staff and students of the Boston School for Deaf Mutes posed for this photo in June 1871. AGB is at the far right of the top row. Unlike many teachers of the time, he was gentle and patient. He would explain how vibrations make sound waves, which produce vibrations in the ears of hearing people. AGB let the children touch his throat so they could "feel" his voice, and he used balloons and feathers to show them the vibrations their voices made.

AGB was always short of money because he spent so much on equipment for his experiments. Whenever he could, he gave private lessons.

Mr. A. Graham Bell's Card of Terms.

PRIVATE INSTRUCTION.

Vocal Physiology, Defects of Speech, Elocution, &c.

A Single Lesson in any department, $5.00

A Course of Twelve Lessons, $50.00

INSTRUCTION OF THE DEAF IN SPEECH,

Including the general education of very young pupils,

Per Annum, $500.00

TEACHERS OF THE DEAF AND DUMB,

Including the mastery of Visible Speech, with the privilege of attending the Deaf Classes, and learning practically the methods of instruction,

The Complete Course,

In cases where Teachers can spend the terms

Per Week,

Per M

"Mr. Watson — Come here"

An invention that would transmit speech, such as the telephone, wasn't really on AGB's mind while he experimented with sound. Instead, he was working on a telegraph that could carry more than one message at the same time.

AGB never stopped thinking about his experiments, even when he was on vacation. While visiting his parents in Brantford during the summer of 1874, AGB once again thought about how singing into a piano causes the strings to vibrate. In his experiments in Boston, he had also noticed that sound could make a metal disk vibrate, and he knew that these disks could make or break electric circuits. Suddenly AGB realized that vibrations from the human voice could move very thin metal disks, and these could change electric currents. He had thought of a way to transmit and receive speech over electric wires!

Knowing how was one thing, but actually sending speech was another. Back in Boston AGB continued working on his experiments. In January 1875 he hired Thomas Watson to help him. Six months later they were hard at work when a reed got stuck in Watson's equipment. Watson tried to free the reed. As he did, AGB heard a ping from his transmitter. It was the first time sound had been transmitted by electricity. AGB hadn't yet transmitted speech, but he was on the right track.

AGB and Watson made their big breakthrough on March 10, 1876. AGB was in one room with his latest transmitter, Watson was in another room with a receiver. AGB accidentally spilled acid on his pants and shouted into the mouthpiece, "Mr. Watson — Come here — I want to see you." Seconds later, in raced Watson. He had heard AGB's voice over the wire: AGB had sent the first telephone message. He celebrated by doing a Mohawk war dance.

This transmitter (top) and receiver (bottom) carried the first words transmitted by telephone. "Telephone" comes from the Greek tele for "far off" and phone for "sound."

Thomas Watson made the equipment for AGB's many experiments and provided the electrical know-how AGB needed.

Here is my lab in Boston, where I transmitted the first words by telephone.

AGB made this sketch the night before he sent the first telephone message.

This is the patent for the telephone, probably the most valuable patent ever.

Brantford Calling

AGB used a transmitter like this one to test the telephone over long distances.

are informed by the *Expositor* that at a at the residence of Professor A. Melville antford, on Friday evening, a rare treat rded to the guests in the experimental ons made by Prof. A. Graham Bell, of the new system of telephony vented by that gentleman. were placed, one in the porch of and the other in an outhouse on and communication between ten miles of wire. Musical n voice, and songs ne instrument the instrume this inven an be c ear , pro too, any of t over one abli ney have a ctly ce can pass hearer at s said, eaker.

Sending messages from one room to another wasn't enough for AGB. The real test of the telephone was to get it to work over longer distances. So when AGB went home to Brantford for his summer vacation in 1876, he brought his telephone with him.

On August 3, 1876, he rode to Mount Pleasant, about 8 km (5 mi.) from Brantford. He set up his receiver in the telegraph office, and people crowded in. AGB nervously sent a telegram to Brantford — the telephone only worked one way — announcing that he was ready. Suddenly he heard voices on the line. Sometimes the words were faint and unclear but they were there. The first call was a success.

The next night AGB's parents were having important dinner guests, and AGB wanted to impress them. He decided to set up a telephone line between Brantford and the Bell home, about 6 km (4 mi.) apart. That meant running a wire from the house to the nearest telegraph line, a distance of about 400 m (¼ mi.). And it had to be done by dinnertime.

AGB strung the wire along fences toward the telegraph line. But then the fences ended. So he convinced a boy to scramble through a tunnel under a road with the wire. The wire was connected just in time, and the Bells' guests were amazed to hear people in Brantford reading and singing.

AGB wanted to test the telephone over an even longer distance. He wrote to the Dominion Telegraph Company and asked to use their line between Brantford and Paris, Ontario, about 13 km (8 mi.) away. The official who received the letter threw it out, but at the last minute his assistant rescued it. AGB got permission to use the line for one hour, at 8:00 P.M. on August 10.

AGB was 29 when he conducted his three telephone tests in Brantford.

> Messy? Maybe.
> But my notes
> helped me prove
> I was the first to
> invent the
> telephone.

AGB set up his receiver in the Paris telegraph office. Soon so many people had gathered in the shop that the door had to be locked. At 8:00 AGB nervously put his ear to the receiver. He heard something, but it was very faint. What was wrong? Quickly AGB sent a telegram to Brantford suggesting adjustments to the transmitter:

> *Can hear faintly "Maple Leaf." Key of D. Words indistinguishable. Disturbance on line. Instruct operator there to change the electromagnet coils on their instrument from low resistance to high resistance.*

Success! The voices boomed out. The Brantford people sang into the transmitter until their throats hurt. Although they were on the line for over three hours, the telegraph company never sent a bill.

THE CHRONOLOGY OF THE TELEPHONE

AGB's father told him that he couldn't attend the telephone test from Brantford to Paris because he had an appointment. Then he surprised AGB by taking part. AGB was amazed to hear his father's voice over the telephone.

Mabel Hubbard

"I did not like him. He was tall and dark, with jet black hair and eyes but dressed badly and carelessly in an old-fashioned suit … he seemed hardly a gentleman." — Mabel describing her first meeting with AGB

Soon after this picture was taken Mabel Hubbard was stricken with scarlet fever. The inflammation spread to her inner ears and left her totally hearing impaired. But Mabel was very smart and became an expert lip-reader, which was rare at the time.

Because Mabel's inner ears had been destroyed, she never got dizzy or seasick. When she was young, she danced by feeling musical vibrations through the soles of her feet.

One of the most important women in AGB's life was Mabel Hubbard. In 1863, when she was five, she became totally hearing impaired. At that time, most hearing-impaired children received almost no education. But Mabel's father was determined that she would be well educated and speak clearly. He sent Mabel to a special school in Germany, then helped open the Clarke School for the Deaf in Massachusetts so that Mabel could go to a school closer to home. Still, her speech was difficult to understand. When Mabel was 15, her father sent her to Boston's best vocal coach, Alexander Graham Bell.

At first, Mabel didn't like her new teacher — she thought he was odd. But as she made progress and he praised her voice, she changed her mind. Teacher and student began to go for walks together. When walking at night, they had to dash from streetlamp to streetlamp — Mabel needed the light to read AGB's lips. AGB began to think of marriage. But he worried that he was too old to marry Mabel because he was ten years older than she was. Mabel's parents thought she was too young to marry, too, and her sisters teased her because AGB spoke so precisely.

Eventually AGB won over Mabel's family, and in 1877 AGB and Mabel were married. She became his lifelong companion.

Mabel shared AGB's love of inventing and acquired a much better grasp of science than most other women of the time. She even supported AGB's work with her own money. Here she is with AGB and their two daughters, Elsie (left) and Marian, known as Daisy (middle).

Mabel was a beautiful dancer!

Here is Mabel in her mid-sixties. From 1910, she helped women fight for the right to vote in the United States.

Life with the Telephone

"This telephone has too many shortcomings to be seriously considered as a means of communication. The device is inherently of no value to us."

— Western Union memo, 1876

Hoy, Hoy!

The telephone was brand-new technology and people didn't trust it. Did it carry disease? Could others on the line hear you? AGB fought a tough battle to have the telephone accepted. He gave lectures about his new invention and demonstrated it to many people, including Queen Victoria. AGB didn't think the queen was holding the receiver correctly so he touched her hand to get her attention. He'd forgotten that no one is allowed to touch the queen. Fortunately she was so excited by the telephone that she didn't notice.

AGB also had to fight in court, this time to maintain his claim that he was the inventor of the telephone. There were lots of challengers who said they had invented it first or, worse, that AGB had stolen the idea. It took 18 years for AGB to win his battle.

Other inventors tried to claim the telephone because the rights to it were so valuable. How valuable? AGB and his partners wanted to raise money, so they offered the rights to the telephone to the Western Union Telegraph Company for $100 000. Western Union said no. A few years later the company would have happily paid millions, but it was too late. AGB and his partners had realized the value of the telephone.

Elisha Gray was one of the men who claimed to have invented the telephone first. But AGB used his lab notes and letters written to his family to prove his claim.

When a telephone line between New York and Chicago officially opened in 1892, AGB made the first call. Actually, AGB hated how telephone calls interrupted his work and refused to have one in his study. And when he answered the phone, he never said, "Hello." Instead he said, "Hoy, Hoy!"

This telephone booth was used by the Chicago police in 1881. Watson created the first telephone booth when he couldn't hear AGB at the other end of the line during a telephone demonstration. He draped blankets over a barrel hoop and crawled underneath.

EVERY MAN, WOMAN and CHILD SHOULD CAREFULLY EXAMINE THE WORKINGS OF PROF. BELL'S Speaking and Singing Telephone, In its practical work of conveying INSTANTANEOUS COMMUNICATION BY DIRECT SOUND so that the person speaking can other end of the line.

Helen Keller (H E L E N   K E L L E R)

AGB knew many important people — kings, queens, scientists — but probably his most famous friend was Helen Keller. She was born on June 27, 1880, in Tuscumbia, Alabama. At 19 months, she became very sick and was left without hearing or sight. Not being able to communicate with people made her angry and frustrated, and she threw frightening temper tantrums.

When Helen was six, her father took her to meet AGB, hoping that he could help Helen. AGB suggested they might find a teacher for Helen at a school for the visually impaired in Boston. There Helen met Annie Sullivan, who finally taught her how to communicate with other people.

Helen loved animals. She liked patting them and feeling their fur.

Helen had an extremely good sense of smell. Some people said she could even tell the color of a rose by its scent!

Helen later wrote a book about her life and dedicated it to AGB. She loved him because he didn't think of her as handicapped. AGB's support helped her to raise money for people with disabilities. When she died in 1968 she was also famous for her work to improve human rights.

Many hearing-impaired people use American Sign Language (ASL) to communicate. ASL requires two hands, so Helen couldn't use it; she needed one hand free to read lips or feel the letters the other person was signing. Instead she used a one-hand manual alphabet. AGB learned this alphabet (shown below) and Braille so that he could communicate with Helen.

Here Helen is communicating with AGB and Annie Sullivan, her teacher. Since Helen was hearing and visually impaired she "heard" by feeling Annie's mouth move and "spoke" to AGB using a one-hand manual alphabet (above).

Beinn Bhreagh

Beginning in 1885, AGB and his family spent summers in the village of Baddeck on Bras d'Or Lake on Cape Breton Island, Nova Scotia. AGB loved the area because it reminded him of Scotland. So the Bells bought a point of land on Bras d'Or Lake and named it Beinn Bhreagh (pronounced Ben Vree-ah), which means "beautiful mountain" in Gaelic, a Scottish language.

Beinn Bhreagh became the site of many of AGB's new experiments. But it was also a place where he could relax — and have food served the way he liked. He preferred plain plates because he'd once had to eat off plates decorated with insects and felt as if he was eating bugs with every bite. He also liked to use glass straws to drink liquids, including tea and soup. Only at Beinn Bhreagh would Mabel allow his odd eating habits.

When he wanted to work, AGB would retreat to his houseboat, the *Mabel of Beinn Bhreagh*. Late at night he would go for a swim and think while he floated.

The house at Beinn Bhreagh had towers, porches, wings, gables, dormers, balconies and 11 fireplaces. On the property were houses for staff, stables, a lab, a dairy, a windmill, 19 km (12 mi.) of roads and more. AGB often slept out in the open porch above the main porch. He also liked to walk in the cool of the night, especially if there were storms.

"*Nothing is done without him; no detail relating to our enjoyment, comfort or safety escapes him. He is forever on the go. At night when all are sleeping he paddles about … When a high wind is blowing or the boat is to be moved he is up, no matter how early the hour, directing, arranging everything.*"

— Mabel writing about AGB at Beinn Bhreagh

AGB loved to play with his grandchildren. At Beinn Bhreagh, he always wore knickerbockers because they were more comfortable than regular pants.

The *Mabel of Beinn Bhreagh*

Baddeck — that's where I built Beinn Bhreagh.

Baddeck

Cape Breton Island

NOVA SCOTIA

ATLANTIC OCEAN

Other Work and Inventions

"Discoveries and inventions arise from the observation of little things."

— AGB discussing his life's work

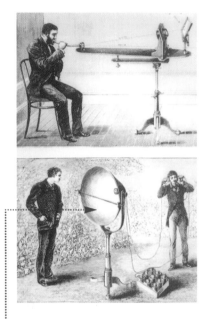

AGB considered the photophone his greatest invention. This device sent sound waves over beams of light. The photophone didn't carry sound over long distances and it only worked when the Sun was shining, but AGB still thought it had great potential.

Whether AGB was in Boston or Beinn Bhreagh, he was inventing. When U.S. president James Garfield was shot in 1881, AGB invented two machines to try to find the bullet. The bullet was too deep and Garfield died, but one of AGB's detectors, the telephonic probe, saved many lives during World War I.

While AGB was trying to save Garfield, Mabel gave birth to a son who died because of weak lungs. So AGB invented a machine to help with breathing. This "vacuum jacket" used suction to move the chest. Improved and renamed the iron lung, it helped people with polio, a paralyzing disease.

In 1880 France had awarded AGB a prize for inventing the telephone. He used the prize money to set up a lab in Washington, D.C. There he improved Thomas Edison's phonograph (an ancestor of the CD player). Edison, who also invented the lightbulb, was not happy that someone had tried to make his invention better.

In 1897 AGB became president of the National Geographic Society. The society published a magazine, but few people bought it because it was so dull. Mabel suggested that AGB add photos. He did and subscriptions soared. Sometimes AGB wrote for the magazine using the name H. A. Largelamb — rearrange the letters and you get A. Graham Bell. In 1898 AGB also became a regent of the Smithsonian Institution, which means he helped to run it.

AGB especially liked to invent flying toys.

What else did AGB do? He:

- invented the audiometer, a device for testing hearing
- suggested devices for measuring water depth and locating icebergs
- invented a system of air conditioning
- suggested the method of using radium to treat deep cancers
- invented a surveying device for finding levels using a water hose
- invented many toys, but was too embarrassed to have them patented

Distilling devices, invented by AGB, turned salty seawater into drinking water.

> A "decibel" is a unit for measuring sound. The Latin "dec" tells you that it's a tenth of a "bel," as in Alexander Graham.

AGB worked on a device that would turn the moisture in breath into drinking water. He thought it would be especially useful to shipwrecked sailors.

Here are AGB's notes and sketch of the vacuum jacket.

Silver Dart

"I believe that it will be possible in a very few years for a person to take his dinner in New York at 7 or 8 o'clock in the evening and eat his breakfast in either Ireland or England the following morning." — AGB

When AGB was a boy in Scotland, he dreamed of flying like a bird. At Beinn Bhreagh he finally had time to experiment with flight. He started with kites made of tetrahedrons, or pyramid shapes, covered with silk. They were light but very strong, especially if he combined several tetrahedrons, or cells as he called them. One of his kites had over 3000 cells.

By the fall of 1903 AGB began to worry that someone else might be first to get a flying machine airborne. He was right: on December 17, Orville and Wilbur Wright became the first people to put a plane into the air. Although he was disappointed, AGB continued working on his own design for a flying machine.

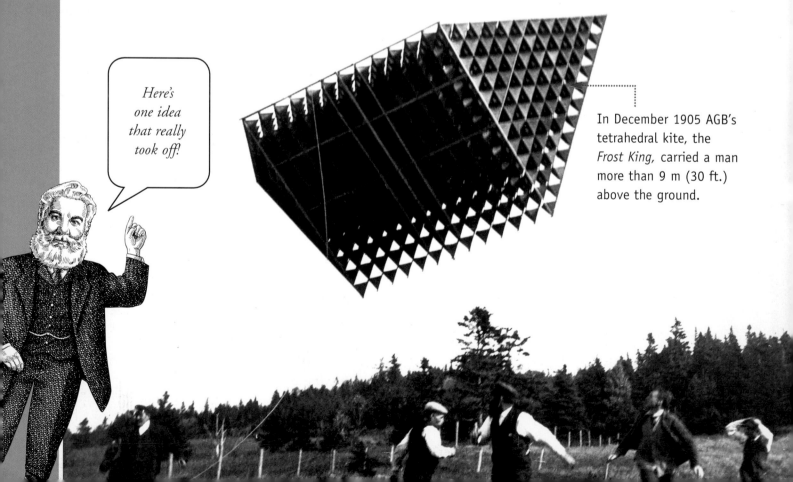

Here's one idea that really took off!

In December 1905 AGB's tetrahedral kite, the *Frost King,* carried a man more than 9 m (30 ft.) above the ground.

In October 1907 AGB hired four young men interested in flight and formed the Aerial Experiment Association (AEA). First they worked on AGB's kite, the *Cygnet*. On December 6, 1907, with a man inside, the kite climbed more than 50 m (165 ft.) into the air.

In Hammondsport, NY, they tested a plane called *Red Wing*. It flew nearly 91 m (300 ft.) and set a record for the first public flight in North America (the Wright brothers' flight was private). Two months later, the AEA's next plane, *White Wing*, flew a record-setting 300 m (1000 ft.). This plane had hinged wing tips to improve stability. Today's planes still have this hinge system, but on the rear edge of the wing.

The AEA's most successful airplane (AGB called them aerodromes) was the *Silver Dart*. On February 23, 1909, they tested it at Beinn Bhreagh. This was the first airplane flight in Canada and the British Empire.

The Aerial Experiment Association included (left to right), Glenn Curtiss, Casey Baldwin, AGB, Thomas Selfridge and Douglas McCurdy. The planes they built are called biplanes. "Bi" means two — these planes had two sets of wings. Most World War I planes were based on AEA designs.

The *Silver Dart*

On July 7, 1908, AGB tested this ring kite.

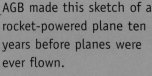

AGB made this sketch of a rocket-powered plane ten years before planes were ever flown.

Final Experiments

AGB's hydrodromes had slanted blades arranged like ladders on the hull. These lifted the hydrodrome out of the water when it began to move quickly. (The blades were curved the same way airplane wings are to give a plane lift.) Mabel tried driving the *HD-4*, but AGB never rode in it.

Despite failing health in his seventies, AGB continued to be interested in the world around him. During a trip to the Bahamas in 1922 he even took part in an undersea exploration.

AGB never stopped working on behalf of hearing-impaired people. In 1887 he opened the Volta Bureau, a research center on hearing impairment. Three years later AGB founded the American Association for the Promotion of the Teaching of Speech to the Deaf. Today it is called the Alexander Graham Bell Association for the Deaf.

On January 25, 1915, AGB made the first coast-to-coast telephone call. From New York, he called his long-ago assistant, Thomas Watson, in San Francisco. "Mr. Watson — Come here — I want to see you," were AGB's words. But this time it would have taken Watson about a week to join him!

At Beinn Bhreagh, AGB began to work on building a hydrofoil, a boat that travels over water, rather than through it. AGB and co-inventor Casey Baldwin called their versions hydrodromes. In 1919 their hydrodrome *HD-4* set a world record for water speed, reaching more than 112 km/h (70 m.p.h.).

During his life, AGB was awarded 24 medals and 12 honorary degrees. But he didn't invent for the honor or the money. "The inventor is a man who looks around upon the world and is not contented with things as they are," AGB once said. "He wants to improve whatever he sees, he wants to benefit the world ..."

"One would think I had never done anything worthwhile but the telephone. That is because it is a money-making invention. It is a pity so many people make money the criterion of success. I wish my experiences had resulted in enabling the deaf to speak with less difficulty. That would have made me truly happy." — AGB

AGB was always busy writing observations about his experiments, notes about events at Beinn Bhreagh or letters to his family. His daughter Daisy married David Fairchild, a famous botanist — Fairchild Tropical Garden in Florida is named after him. AGB's other daughter, Elsie, traveled widely with her husband, Gilbert Grosvenor, editor of *National Geographic*.

AGB died August 2, 1922, at age 75 at Beinn Bhreagh, with Mabel holding his hand. He was buried on a hill overlooking Bras d'Or Lake, wearing the knickerbockers that he always wore there, in a plain wooden coffin lined with airplane silk. During AGB's funeral, telephone service in North America was halted for one minute.

AGB's Life at a Glance

1847   March 3 — Alexander Graham Bell is born in Edinburgh, Scotland

1857   November 25 — Mabel Hubbard is born in Cambridge, Massachusetts

1858   AGB enrolls at the Royal High School, Edinburgh

1862   AGB moves to London to live with his grandfather

1867   May 17 — AGB's younger brother, Edward, dies of tuberculosis

1868   May — AGB begins teaching hearing-impaired children in London

October — AGB begins studying at the University of London

1870   May 28 — AGB's older brother, Melville, dies of tuberculosis

July 21 — AGB and his parents sail to Canada. They arrive August 1.

1871   April — AGB begins teaching at the Boston School for Deaf Mutes

1872   AGB trains teachers of hearing-impaired children

1873   AGB is appointed professor of Vocal Physiology and Elocution at Boston University

1874   July — While visiting his family in Brantford, AGB realizes how the telephone could work

1875   January — AGB hires Thomas Watson as an assistant

June 2 — A sticking reed in AGB's apparatus leads to telephone experiments

1876   March 7 — A patent for the telephone is issued to AGB

March 10 — First telephone message, Boston

June 25 — First public display of the telephone, Philadelphia

August 3 — First telephone call between two villages, from Brantford to Mount Pleasant, about 8 km (5 mi.)

August 4 — Telephone call from Brantford to the Bell home, about 6 km (4 mi.)

August 10 — Telephone call from Brantford to Paris, Ontario, 13 km (8 mi.)

October 6 — First two-way conversation, between AGB and Watson

1877   July 11 — AGB marries Mabel Hubbard

1878   May 8 — AGB's first child, Elsie May, is born

1880   February 15 — AGB's second daughter, Marian (Daisy), is born

April 1 — AGB invents the photophone

September — France awards Bell the Volta Prize and $10 000 for the invention of the telephone. He uses the money to set up the Volta Laboratory.

1881 July-August — AGB attempts to locate a bullet lodged in President Garfield's body. He is unsuccessful and Garfield dies.

August 15 — AGB's son Edward is born but dies within hours

Summer-Fall — AGB develops a vacuum jacket, a machine to help people with weak lungs breathe

1883 October — AGB opens a school for hearing-impaired children in Washington, D.C.

November 17 — AGB's son Robert is born but doesn't survive

1885 Summer — AGB and family visit Baddeck, Nova Scotia, for the first time

1887 AGB and associates patent the graphophone, an improvement on Thomas Edison's phonograph

AGB meets Helen Keller

1890 AGB helps found American Association for the Promotion of the Teaching of Speech to the Deaf and becomes its first president

1892 AGB begins to build at Beinn Bhreagh

1895 AGB begins experiments with flight

1897 AGB becomes president of the National Geographic Society

1898 AGB becomes a regent of the Smithsonian Institution

1907 October 1 — The Aerial Experiment Association (AEA) is formed

December 6 — The flight of the kite, the *Cygnet*

1908 March 12 — The flight of the *Red Wing*, the first powered flight by the AEA and the first public flight in North America

May 19 — The *White Wing* flies a record-setting 300 m (1000 ft.)

1909 February 23 — The *Silver Dart* makes the first powered heavier-than-air flight in Canada

1911 AGB builds a hydrodrome, called the *HD-1*, but it breaks apart in trials

1912 October-December — Trials with the *HD-2*

1913 AGB develops the *HD-3*

1915 January 25 — AGB opens the telephone line from New York to San Francisco

1919 September 9 — The *HD-4* sets a world marine speed record. It reaches speeds of more than 112 km/h (70 m.p.h.).

1922 August 2 — AGB dies at Beinn Bhreagh

1923 January 3 — Mabel dies. She is buried beside AGB at Beinn Bhreagh.

Quite a life, wasn't it?

Visit AGB

Bell Homestead
National Historic Site
94 Tutela Heights Road
Brantford, Ontario
Tour the house where AGB
and his parents first lived in
Canada. Inside you'll find
paintings by AGB's mother,
replicas of early telephones
and AGB's bedroom.

Alexander Graham Bell
National Historic Site
Baddeck, Nova Scotia
The museum here has displays
on AGB's life and many of his
inventions. You'll see AGB's
equipment, including the
original hydrodrome *HD-4*. You
can see Beinn Bhreagh, AGB's
home, from the museum.

Smithsonian Institution
Washington, D.C.
AGB was a regent of the
Smithsonian Institution. The
institution also has a number of
his telephones.

All of these places have web sites, too!

Index